Scarborough Castle

Few visitors to Scarborough can fail to be aware of the Castle. The massive headland of Castle Hill, at its highest point over 300 ft above sea level and 100 ft above the town, separates the North and South Bays. From the South Bay and the harbour, the Castle's curtain wall encrusts the skyline; from the North Bay and beyond, it is the tower of the keep that stands out, like a ruined lighthouse.

Any history of Castle Hill must begin at a time long before the castle was built. Excavations have shown that there was a prehistoric settlement on the eastern, or seaward, side of the headland, and this same spot was later chosen for a Roman signal station.

Castle Hill is a wedge-shaped block, with precipitous cliffs on the north and east sides. On the west side a narrow neck connects it with the mainland, and on the south-west side the steep ravine known as Castle Dykes marks the line of a fault, or fracture, in the rocks on which Scarborough stands. Two more faults, originally pointed out by William Smith, the Father of English Geology, cross the neck of land below the Castle's barbican. These faults resulted in a great block of tough grit and limestone being dropped into the softer rocks which have now been excavated by the sea into North and South Bays. So Castle Hill stands out like a clenched fist on this stretch of coast, protecting the harbour and the town behind it.

D1245324

*Left: The interior of the keep
seen through the gap made by
bombardment during the Civil War*

An aerial view across Castle Hill to the sea. In the middle foreground are the defences of the barbican, and in the centre of the picture is the keep and inner bailey. At the cliff edge can be seen the remains of the Roman signal station and medieval chapel

Early History

The first identifiable settlers on the headland date back to the early Iron Age. From the remains found in about 50 small rubbish pits that were excavated in the 1920s, they seem to have come from the lower Rhine area. The excavations yielded flint tools as well as late Bronze Age implements, axes and chisel, rings, a bracelet and pins, all of which can be seen in the local museums.* Among other significant finds were some of the wattle and daub used to build huts, some beads of glass and amber, and a ring of jet. Right up until the nineteenth century jet has been made into jewellery on the North Yorkshire coast. Perhaps it was some small recompense for the settlers at a time when, away from the coast, the land was wet, wooded and generally inhospitable.

An Iron Age cookpot from Castle Hill

Remains from Castle Hill are in the Rotunda Museum, Vernon Road, and Londesborough Lodge in The Crescent.

The Romans

Some 700 to 800 years later, after much of Britain had been occupied by the Romans, Castle Hill became the site of a signal station. A chain of these stations, at Huntcliff, Goldsborough, Ravenscar, Scarborough and Filey, was set up between the Tees and Flamborough Head to give warning of the approach of hostile ships. The warning, by smoke signal, could then be passed along the coast or inland to garrisons like that at Malton (Derventio). For this was after about 370 AD, and late in the Roman occupation; already the edges of the Empire were beginning to crumble. The signal stations remained in commission until at least 394, but the Roman forces that backed them up were finally withdrawn by 410, and the undefended coasts were again open to attack by raiders. Intended more as look-out posts than forts, the stations and their small garrisons may well have been over-run before the end of the fourth century. In excavations at Huntcliff, fourteen skeletons of men, women and children, were found in a well. At the next signal station, Goldsborough, a skull with sword clefts was found, and a skeleton huddled against a wall.

A small 4th century bowl with painted decoration, found on Castle Hill

A 'Mickle Bale'

Within the ditch and bank of the signal station lie the remains of later buildings. The earliest of these was a chapel which made use of part of the ruined wall of the station. It dates from about the year 1000, by which time there was a fishing settlement around the harbour below Castle Hill. Scarborough's name is believed to come from the tenth-century settlement or *burh* of Kormak and Thorgils, nicknamed Skarthi or Harelip, described in the Old Norse *Kormakssaga.*

In 1066 Scarborough was the landing place of Harald Hardrada and Tostig before they sailed up the Humber and Ouse to eventual defeat at Stamford Bridge. The town was sacked. According to Norse saga, a 'mickle bale', or huge bonfire, was lit on Castle Hill, and its brands used to burn down the houses below one after another. The town may well have suffered a second burning in the 'Harrying of the North', when William the Conqueror put down a rebellion with Viking ferocity. Certainly Scarborough gets no separate mention in the Domesday Survey of 1086, though it may be included in the entry for Falsgrave, an ancient pre-Norman manor which once belonged to Tostig and is today an area of Scarborough.

Part of a saga manuscript (Snorri Sturluson, 1178–1241). The names Kliflond (Cleveland) and Skardaborg (Scarborough) occur in lines 7 and 9

SCARBOROUGH BOROUGH COUNCIL

The Norman Castle

The first castle at Scarborough probably had its beginnings in the troubled reign of Stephen. The sovereign's power was wielded locally by William le Gros, Earl of Albermarle, who became Earl of Yorkshire after defeating the Scots in the Battle of the Standard at Northallerton in 1138. Scarborough became one of his main strongholds. He had a ditch dug across the narrowest part of the headland, fortified it, and rebuilt the Chapel of St. Catherine on the site of the earlier chapel.

The entrance and principal structure of this early castle was a gate-tower which stood astride the line of the curtain wall somewhere near where the keep now stands. It was pulled down after 1155 when the castle was taken over by the Crown. Henry II, who had come to the throne in 1154, was quick to adopt a policy of reducing the power which had fallen into the hands of the barons during the previous years of anarchy. Le Gros at first refused to yield Scarborough, and when he eventually surrendered the castle to the King it was in poor condition. Henry put the castle in the charge of Roger, Archbishop of York, as its first Governor, and had the fortifications strengthened. The Great Keep was built between 1158 and 1168, and an inner bailey was made by running a ditch and bank across the angle of the headland so as to enclose the keep.

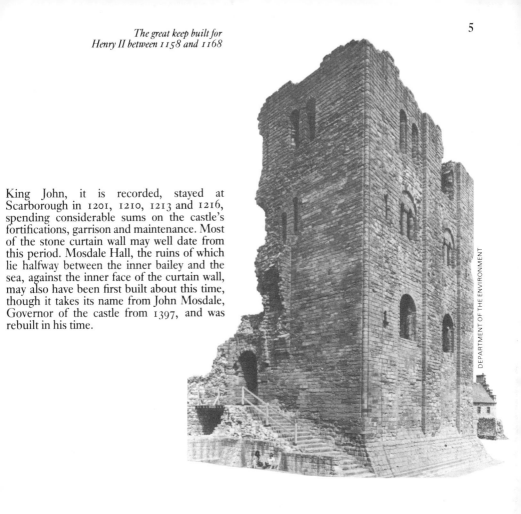

*The great keep built for
Henry II between 1158 and 1168*

DEPARTMENT OF THE ENVIRONMENT

King John, it is recorded, stayed at Scarborough in 1201, 1210, 1213 and 1216, spending considerable sums on the castle's fortifications, garrison and maintenance. Most of the stone curtain wall may well date from this period. Mosdale Hall, the ruins of which lie halfway between the inner bailey and the sea, against the inner face of the curtain wall, may also have been first built about this time, though it takes its name from John Mosdale, Governor of the castle from 1397, and was rebuilt in his time.

*The curtain wall, seen from the
harbour, crowns the steep slope
of Castle Hill*

DEPARTMENT OF THE ENVIRONMENT

Siege and Surrender

Henry III, from a tomb effigy

NATIONAL PORTRAIT GALLERY

Under Henry III and Edward I there was more building at Scarborough. But the castle, on its exposed site, was always expensive to maintain. Henry III gave orders for completing a great gateway in 1243-5, and Edward I held court at Scarborough in 1275 and 1280, but in 1278 it was recorded that the castle's condition had so deteriorated that roofs, the wooden bridge between barbican and main gate, and 1100 yards of curtain wall had collapsed.

Edward's Welsh hostages were imprisoned in the castle in 1295, and in 1311 there were Scottish prisoners from Stirling. In 1312 the castle became the refuge of Piers Gaveston, Earl of Cornwall and the favourite of Edward II. His influence on that King did not endear him to the leading barons, whom he further angered by giving them nicknames. A number of them, prompted by the Earl of Lancaster, laid siege to the castle. Gaveston defended stoutly, but his provisions ran out and he was forced to surrender on terms of safe conduct. These terms turned out to be worth little when he was conducted to Deddington Castle in Oxfordshire; one of his chief enemies, the Earl of Warwick, had him seized from there and beheaded.

The siege of 1312 was the first of several the castle was to undergo. It needed a great many repairs over the years that followed. After the Scottish victory at Bannockburn in 1314, Northumberland, Durham and even Yorkshire were under threat from raiders.

Edward I, from a manuscript in the British Library

BRITISH LIBRARY

Capture and Re-capture

Richard III, a visitor to Scarborough during his short reign (1483–5)

'Tudor' map of Scarborough, undated but possibly as early as 1485. From a manuscriunt in the British Museum

Edward III's ambitions lay in France rather than in Scotland. During the Hundred Years' War the importance of Scarborough to England's wool trade with the Continent brought castle and town into the struggles from time to time. The castle's outermost defences were improved, but otherwise it is the same story of decay; in 1393 it was stated that the castle could not be restored for less than £2000, and between 1396 and 1400, following further inquiry into its defensive condition, repairs had to be carried out.

The castle again entertained its lord in 1484, when Richard III visited Scarborough. One of the towers along the curtain wall was named the Queen's Tower after Anne, his queen.

Trouble with the French and Scots occurred again in Henry VIII's reign. But in the North the rising known as 'The Pilgrimage of Grace' posed a more serious threat to the Crown. Protesters against religious change, dismayed at plans to suppress the monasteries, mustered an army under Robert Aske. According to one account Scarborough Castle was under siege for 20 days, but this story may have been put about by the Constable, Sir Ralph Eure. In 1537 he was himself accused of plundering the castle by stripping lead from the towers to make a brewery vessel, and of cheating the garrison of their wages. In 1538 repairs to the castle were planned, though it is unlikely that much was done about its generally decayed state.

Scarborough Castle changed hands twice in 1557, during the reign of Mary. In April of that year Sir Thomas Stafford, who himself claimed royal descent from Edward III, saw in the marriage of Mary to Philip of Spain an opportunity to rally popular support against foreign influence. Landing on the Yorkshire coast he captured the castle by cunning rather than force. With no more than about 30 men, disguised as peasants visiting the market, he was able to seize the sentries and admit the whole troop with their concealed weapons. The exploit gave rise to a local saying that 'a Scarborough warning is a word and a blow, but the blow first'! Stafford proclaimed himself Protector of the whole realm, but his occupation of Scarborough Castle lasted less than a week. It was retaken without loss by Lord Westmorland, and Stafford was executed for treason.

Though some repairs were carried out in 1581-4, by 1619 it was recorded that the castle was so ruinous it could scarcely be repaired for £4000, and later that year it was granted by James I to John, Earl of Holderness.

8

The CASTLE & Town of Scarborough, as they appear a

This Castle, first built by Will.ᵐ le Groſse, Earl of A...
Stephen, was rebuilt in a more ſplendid manner, & t...

Samuel Buck's engraving of
Scarborough's South Bay and
the castle

of a mile from the *SPAW*

...e, in y time of King
> by King Hen.y 2.d

The Civil War

At the start of the Civil War in 1642 the town of Scarborough was one of the Parliamentary side's most northerly outposts. The Earl of Essex, head of the Parliamentary forces, commissioned Sir Hugh Cholmley, a local landowner and member of Parliament, to raise a regiment of foot and to quarter it at Scarborough. The castle at this time belonged to one Francis Thompson, a burgher more disposed to support the King (Charles I) than the Parliamentary cause. With some reluctance he handed over the keys to Sir Hugh, who declared that he had 'noe other end than to preserve the libertie of the subject and to render the duties to his Majestie'.

Sir Hugh Cholmley was convinced, as were many others, that the struggle between King and Parliament would soon be over. He personally urged Parliament to make a peace and come to a treaty with the King. There was no response to his appeal and neither did he receive any money from Parliament to support the force he had gathered on their behalf. Gradually he became disaffected with their cause, and after the battle of Edgehill, in October 1642, he became convinced that Parliament would never come to terms with the King. At the same time friends of the Queen (Henrietta Maria) were urging Sir Hugh to quit Parliament on the grounds that it would assist the peace of the county, which was still mostly Royalist. Finally, he asked to speak to the Queen at York, and rode out from Scarborough early on 20 March 1643. Putting a black patch over one eye he reached York without being discovered, and promised to deliver up castle and town to the King.

Returning to Scarborough he sent back his commission to the Earl of Essex, but his letter was intercepted and opened by Sir John Hotham, who was holding Hull for Parliament. Sir John straightaway wrote two letters, one to dissuade Cholmley from quitting Parliament and the other to the Captain of the Guard at Scarborough Castle urging him to prevent his Governor from changing sides. Sir Hugh then disclosed his intentions to the garrison, telling

Sir Hugh Cholmley, Governor of the castle and its defender in the first siege

the soldiers to leave or stay. Only about 20 left, together with the Captain of the Guard who posted off to Hull on a promise that he would secure the release of Captain Browne Bushell, one of Cholmley's officers who had been imprisoned there by Sir John Hotham. Bushell was released, but only on the private condition that he would take the castle back for Parliament. With Sir Hugh again away in York, Bushell landed at Scarborough with some 40 seamen and, late at night, was let into the castle by his brother, a lieutenant in the garrison. His force seized the Captain and turned the soldiers out at the gate.

Word of all this reached Sir Hugh. On his return from York he brought with him a body of Royalist troops from the Earl of Newcastle's forces, and arranged to meet Captain Bushell at the main gate. Faced by the show of force and by reminders of his past loyalty, Bushell agreed to return the castle to Cholmley. As a contemporary source puts it, the castle 'though able to hold out against an army of 10,000 men was thus twice taken in a week without shedding a drop of blood'. Not long after, two pinnaces with men and ammunition arrived from Hull to support Bushell's coup, but these were captured by Sir Hugh before they knew that the castle had changed hands again.

After the Battle of Marston Moor in July 1644, Parliamentary forces under Lord Fairfax began to tighten their grip on the county and moved up to within six miles of the town. Sir Hugh Cholmley sent a list of terms for the surrender of Scarborough direct to Parliament, refusing to treat with Fairfax. There was little likelihood that all his conditions would be met, but the move gained him valuable time to get in crops and supplies and to fortify the town, while Fairfax turned his attention to other military targets. So it was not until January 1645 that Scarborough came under direct threat, this time from a force of 3000 Scots under Sir John Meldrum, a Scottish soldier of fortune.

There was never much doubt that the town's extended defences would eventually be over-

run. Cholmley held the town and harbour until February, but once these had fallen he was cut off in the castle, with neither retreat nor source of supply. For over five months he resisted all the efforts of the besieging force. Batteries of cannon were brought up to pound away at the medieval stonework, and the besiegers even explored the approach from the seaward side. In doing so their leader met with an accident. Sir John 'had his hat blown off, which he labouring to recover, his coat was blown over his head, and, striving to get it down, the wind blew him over, head foremost, down the cliff amongst the rocks and stones att least steeple height'. After this fall he 'lay speechless for 3 days, but in 6 weeks was about again'.

Meldrum's cannon barrage at last succeeded in splitting the tower of the keep in two. The west wall of the tower collapsed and fell to the ground, blocking the path down to the gatehouse, which was in danger of being taken. But the besieging force hesitated, and when they began their assault they were driven back. Stones from the fallen keep were thrown amongst them with great effect. After this the gatehouse was so battered with cannon fire that its garrison had to withdraw. Twice Meldrum's men tried to occupy it, and twice they were repelled. Meldrum himself received a fatal wound. For ten days together the gatehouse lay unheld by either side.

The siege was renewed under Sir Matthew Boynton, member of Parliament for Scarborough. By July disease and shortage of provisions forced Cholmley to consider surrender on terms. Out of his garrison of about 200 men, he recorded in his diary of the siege, 180 were sick, most of them unable to move. Lady Cholmley had stayed throughout to tend the sick and wounded. On 25 July 1645 the castle was given up. After a hole had been cut in the castle wall because the gatehouse had been so 'barracadoed', the garrison, or those that were able to, marched out with drums and banners flying. Sir Hugh left for the Continent. Parliament voted a day of thanksgiving to God, and £5000 to the repair of the castle.

The Final Siege

Sir Matthew Boynton, Member of Parliament for Scarborough, who took over as Governor in 1645

The castle's active days were not over by any means. Sir Matthew Boynton, who had been made Governor on behalf of Parliament, died and was succeeded in the post by his second son, Col. Matthew Boynton. At the start of the second Civil War in 1648, Col. Boynton had a discontented garrison. Money might have been voted for repairs to the castle, but Parliament was well in arrears over pay for the men. Like Sir Hugh Cholmley before him, Boynton found Parliament a difficult master to serve. In July 1648, he rebelled against them and declared for the King.

The Parliamentary forces found themselves having to besiege both town and castle a second time. Town and harbour fell by September 15th, but the castle was again slow to yield. At length, with an exhausted garrison and broken defences, Col. Boynton surrendered the castle to Col. Bethell for Parliament on 15 December 1648. The Council of State for the Commonwealth ordered its demolition in the following year, but it was already badly damaged and the order was never carried out.

From the barbican, the keep shows the damage wrought by Civil War cannon

*Aerial view of Castle Hill from the south-east, with
North Bay in the background, showing the curtain wall,
inner bailey and keep (centre). At the cliff edge on the right
the remains of the Roman signal station can be made out*

SIMPSON PHOTOGRAPHY WHITBY

14

View from the entrance in 1818, showing the drawbridge that then separated the barbican from the rest of the castle

NORTH YORKSHIRE COUNTY LIBRARY

Prison and Barracks

There was still enough of the castle left for it to serve as a prison. Scarborough's best-known prisoner was George Fox, the Quaker, who was imprisoned in the castle in April 1665 for refusing to swear an oath. It was anything but a comfortable prison. After he had put out money, as most prisoners did in those days, to improve his accommodation, he was moved to a worse room where, he wrote, 'I had neither chimney nor fire-hearth. This being to the sea-side and lying much open, the wind drove the rain in forcibly, so that the water came up over my bed and ran about the room that I was fain to skim it up with a platter.' But Fox was not without temporal influence. When Sir Jordan Crosland, Governor of the castle, went to London, one of the King's gentlemen, Esquire Marsh, said he 'would go 100 miles barefoot for George Fox's liberty'. By the order of the Governor George Fox was released in September 1666. The officers and soldiers were impressed by his fortitude: 'he is as stiff as a tree, and as pure as a bell', said one of them, 'for we could never stir him'.

The castle now had little of its former power. Like the nation as a whole it had become un-accustomed to war when, in September 1745, news came that the Young Pretender was marching south into England. A committee of the inhabitants of Scarborough, seriously worried by the 'very defenceless condition' of the town and port, raised money and petitioned for a small garrison. By the end of the following year, although before then the battle of Culloden had put an end to the Jacobite rising, they had got more than they asked. The Master of Ordnance had commissioned new barracks for 120 officers and soldiers in the castle, a powder magazine for the district, and the re-building of the South Steel Battery.

The strengthened gun batteries did not pre-vent Paul Jones, the American pirate, from entering the bay in 1779 and destroying two men-of-war which had been sent to protect merchant vessels. But the threat of French invasion had by then confirmed the need for a permanent garrison, and the continuing conflict with France brought French prisoners of war to the castle in 1796.

The last action seen by the castle also came from the sea. In December 1914 two German battle cruisers, the *Derfflinger* and *Von der Tann* steamed out of the mist to fire over 500 shells into the town and castle, damaging the stone-work and destroying the brick barracks. After the First World War, in 1920, Scarborough Castle was put in the care of the Office of Works, whose successors, the Department of the Environment, now look after castle and headland under the Ancient Monuments Acts.

Supposed portrait of George Fox (1624–1690/1), from a painting at Swarthmore College, USA

SOCIETY OF FRIENDS

Map of Scarborough Castle and Headland

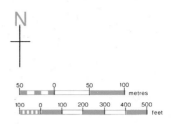

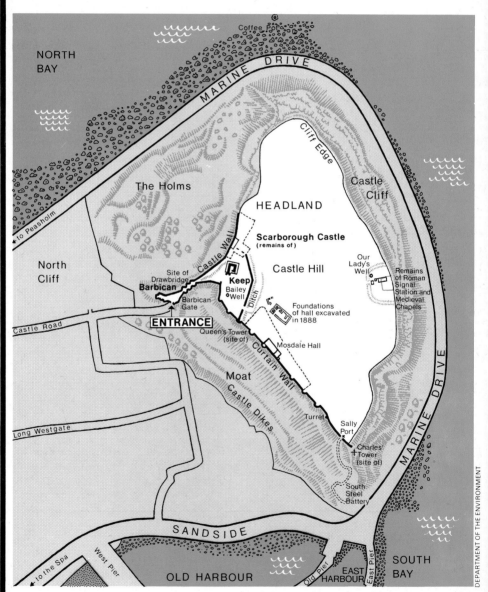

N

50   0   50   100
metres

100   0   100 200 300 400 500
feet

NORTH
BAY

MARINE DRIVE

Coffee Pot

Cliff Edge

The Holms

HEADLAND

Castle Cliff

North
Cliff

Scarborough Castle
(remains of)

Castle Wall

Castle Hill

Our
Lady's
Well

Remains
of Roman
Signal
Station and
Medieval
Chapels

Site of
Drawbridge
Barbican

Keep

Bailey
Well

Ditch

Foundations
of hall excavated
in 1888

to Peasholm

Barbican
Gate

ENTRANCE

Castle Road

Queen's Tower
(site of)

Mosdale Hall

Long Westgate

Moat

Castle Dikes

Curtain Wall

Turret

Sally
Port

Charles'
Tower
(site of)

South
Steel
Battery

to the Spa

West Pier

SANDSIDE

OLD HARBOUR

Old Pier

East Pier

EAST
HARBOUR

SOUTH
BAY

DEPARTMENT OF THE ENVIRONMENT

A Tour of the Castle and Headland

The entrance to the castle is through the fortified gateway of the barbican or outer defence. Within it the path slopes upwards to cross the ditch separating the headland from the mainland by a stone bridge of two arches, which replaces the two wooden drawbridges of earlier times. The path continues to climb, with a reconstructed wall on the left and, to the right, a wall on a steep slope connecting the outer defences with the curtain wall above.

Passing to the left of the keep, follow a grass path across the headland to the cliff edge. The ditch which surrounded the courtyard of the Roman watchtower can be clearly seen, although cliff falls have removed its eastern side. A gateway from the landward side led into the square courtyard in the centre of which stood a high tower 50 ft square at its foundations. The outline can be traced on the ground, and seven bases of wooden posts to support the floor beams of the next storey were found during excavation. Obscuring the outline of the Roman building are the remains of the medieval chapel. The first chapel to be built made use of part of the ruined wall of the Roman signal station, the second, built by William le Gros, was larger and is represented by a stone grave slab on which a shield is carved, and the third had a priest's house attached, parts of which are still visible. The remains of the chapel were included in a later dwelling which was extended to the north. Inside the chancel can be seen a paved circular track which was for a horse-powered mill. A vaulted water tank of medieval date once fed a large pond to the north-northwest, and continued in use, for it shows eighteenth-century repair work. Just by this building, and within the Roman ditch, is the 'Well of Our Lady', held to be miraculous because its water stood within 10 ft of the surface. It now seems to be permanently dry.

Walk southwards along the cliff edge to the point where it is reached by the castle's curtain wall. This was the main defence of the castle on the west and southwest, extending along the whole of the landward side of the headland, and may be based on the work of William le Gros. It has been much patched and repaired, with buttresses and towers added at different dates. The wall formerly ended at the cliff edge with a tower known as the Cockhill or Charles's Tower, in which George Fox was imprisoned in 1665-6. By 1750 it had fallen into the sea, which at that time washed the foot of the cliff.

Not far from the end of the wall is a postern gate or sally port which leads to a steep path with steps descending to the harbour, and from which the remains of the South Steel Battery can be reached. The loopholed wall protecting the outer or western side of the path has been altered in the seventeenth and eighteenth centuries but is medieval in origin.

Continue along the inside of the curtain wall, noting the round-fronted towers which were probably added during the reign of Henry III. The remains of Mosdale Hall, built against the face of the wall between the castle's inner bailey and the sea, were largely exposed when the brickwork barracks built in 1746 on the same site were demolished after damage from German bombardment in the 1914-18 War. They consist of an undercroft, used for storage; the hall itself, with a solar or chamber at the south-eastern end, would have been on the first floor.

Away from the wall, to the right, are the foundations of another medieval hall. The remains were excavated in 1888 and again in 1973. Details of the aisles may be made out, and there were clearly several service rooms at one end.

The inner bailey of the castle is separated from the open headland by a ditch and bank, at first palisaded and later, probably towards the end of the thirteenth century, surmounted by a stone wall. Crossing into the bailey at its south-eastern corner, note just to the right the abutments of an earlier bridge across the ditch.

Ahead rises the keep, seen to its best advantage from this side. It is a fine square Norman keep,

18

*The gateway to
the barbican*

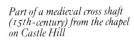

Part of a medieval cross shaft (15th-century) from the chapel on Castle Hill

four storeys high and originally standing to some 100 ft, with a turret at each corner. The west wall was destroyed in the Civil War sieges, and little remains here but the massive sloping base. As was usual in such keeps, entry was at first-floor level. The flight of stone steps against the south wall led into a fore-building which had a dungeon and cesspit in its basement extending under the steps.

The basement of the keep itself was probably used only for storage and was reached by a spiral staircase, the lowest steps of which can be seen in the ruined west wall. A single room occupied the first floor. Spanning it from north to south was a great flying arch carrying the second floor and the wall that divided this into two rooms. Both floors had large round-backed fireplaces in the east wall, and were reached by the west wall staircase, which also served rooms within the thickness of the wall. The garderobes, or latrines, of these rooms discharged through chutes, the remains of which can be made out just above the sloping base of the west wall.

The east wall, though much refaced, is almost complete, and its windows have been restored – pairs on the third floor and more elaborate windows with coupled shafts on the second. The first floor windows would have been similar.

Before leaving the inner bailey it is worth looking at the castle well. It is over 150 ft deep, with a stone lining, Norman work dating from the time of Henry II, for the first 68 ft, below which the sides are of natural rock. Coins and tokens dating from the Civil Wars were recovered from the well and can be seen in the Vernon Road museum.

Return towards the main entrance to see how the castle's defences grew around the neck of land that connects Castle Hill with the mainland. The original entrance to the castle of William le Gros was defended by a gatehouse which must have stood roughly in the mouth of the funnel now formed by the walls that

Second-floor window in the east wall of the keep

The bridge across the great ditch, looking towards North Bay. On the right is the wall of the inner bailey with its beacon basket

DEPARTMENT OF THE ENVIRONMENT

Finds from Castle Hill:
A 16th/17th-century Bellarmine jug

Finds from Castle Hill:
A decorated plate in 16th-
century slipware

descend towards the barbican. These walls are part of an extension of the defences carried out during the reigns of Henry III and Edward I. Where the ditch is now spanned by a stone bridge there were two drawbridges, one of which survived until the last century (see page 14). This was the outer of the two, raised from the twin towers between the two spans of the present bridge. The other was raised from the inner side of the ditch.

Across the ditch lie the outer defences of the barbican. The first mention of a barbican is as early as 1174-5, and remains of a rectangular tower have recently been found within the area enclosed by the present structure. The 'new tower before the Castle Gate' ordered by Henry III in 1243 may have formed part of the existing barbican which has been much repaired and rebuilt over the centuries. These outer defences consist of a fortified gateway with two massive half-round towers and a flanking wall to the west with two smaller towers. A raised platform running behind the wall allowed the approach to the gate to be covered by bowmen or gunners. The gate itself had a portcullis and could be defended from above through the gap between the two recessed arches. The presence of the barbican on the landward side of the ditch served to deny opposing forces the high ground nearest to the castle entrance, which could then have come under fire from primitive artillery. During the later sieges of the Civil Wars the castle was to suffer severe bombardment, but by this time artillery was powerful enough to be effective from more distant positions like the North Cliff and St. Mary's Churchyard.

Outside the gate again, it is worth taking another look at the fortifications as they might have appeared to a besieging force. The most striking impression is of the height advantage the defenders had. There were very few places where an approach could not be detected and action taken against it. To the right, northwards, lie the Holms, a tumbled area of cliff where lime-burning used to take place, while the steep ravine of Castle Dykes going down to the left will take you to the Harbour beneath the most impressive stretch of the curtain wall. The tower topped by an iron beacon basket, and its neighbour to the right, are solid bastions and probably date from the reign of King John. The remainder date mostly from the time of Henry III. The red brick and railings mark the site of the later barracks built after the 1745 rebellion.

It requires a little more imagination to realise how the castle must have looked from the Harbour and seaward side. Turner's water-colour (opposite) helps, and it should be remembered that the Foreshore Road linking Sandside with the Spa and South Cliff is only one hundred years old, while Marine Drive, which links North and South Bays around the headland, was not completed until the early years of this century. But it is still apparent what a fine defensive position the castle occupied on this North Sea coast, rivalling Dover Castle in the way it dominates harbour and hinterland.

Engraving of Scarborough harbour and castle, after a water-colour by J. M. W. Turner RA

*The seal of Scarborough
from a 17th-century
silver badge*

SCARBOROUGH BOROUGH COUNCIL

DEPARTMENT OF THE ENVIRONMENT

On the left the barbican, and on the right the bridge, formerly with two drawbridges, leading into the castle

ACKNOWLEDGMENTS

The pictures on pages 3, 4, 19 (top), 21 and 23 are reproduced by courtesy of the Department of Tourism and Amenities, Scarborough; the objects may be seen in the Rotunda and Crescent Museums. Those on page 6, 7 (bottom) and 8 (top) are reproduced by courtesy of the Trustees of the National Portrait Gallery, the British Library and the British Museum.

The prints on pages 10 and 14 are reproduced by permission of North Yorkshire County Library, and the supposed portrait of George Fox by permission of the Library Committee of the Religious Society of Friends.

The portrait of Sir Matthew Boynton on page 11 was photographed by kind permission of the Burton Agnes Estate Trust.

INFORMATION

Scarborough Castle occupies a central position in the resort. The entrance to castle and headland is reached from the centre of the town by Castle Road, and there is limited car parking close to the entrance.

Grid reference: TA050893. Ordnance Survey map 101 in the 1:50 000 series.

SEASON TICKETS

Season tickets, valid for a year from the date of issue, give admission to ancient monuments and historic buildings looked after by the Department of the Environment, Scottish Office and Welsh Office. The tickets can be bought at many of the monuments, from HMSO bookshops (see back cover), or by direct application to any of the above Departments.

DEPARTMENT OF THE ENVIRONMENT